# My Angry BOOK

Honor
Head

ARCTURUS

Sarah
Ward

This book has been developed in consultation with Clare Arnold, an art psychotherapist with over 30 years of experience of working with child and adolescent mental health issues.

**ARCTURUS**

This edition published in 2024 by Arcturus Publishing Limited
26/27 Bickels Yard, 151–153 Bermondsey Street,
London SE1 3HA

Author: Honor Head
Illustrator: Sarah Ward
Consultant: Clare Arnold
Editor: Violet Peto
Designer: Amy McSimpson
Managing Editor: Joe Harris
Design Manager: Rosie Bellwood-Moyler

ISBN: 978-1-3988-4691-3
CH011793NT
Supplier 13, Date 0524, PI 00007606

Printed in China

This is Little Panda with her family.
Little Panda has lots of different feelings.

This book is about what
happens when Little Panda feels **angry**.

Little Panda is kind and fun to be with.

But sometimes she gets **angry**.

Anger is something that you feel.

People feel angry for lots of reasons.

You might feel angry when you cannot have your own way.

I want to play some more.

You might feel angry when you have to
do things you don't want to ...

... like going to bed ...

I'm not tired!

... or brushing your teeth.

What else might make
Little Panda angry?

Sometimes being angry makes you sulk.
You might cross your arms and **make a face.**

You might **turn your back** and not talk to anyone.

When you are **very, very, angry** you ...

... feel hot in the face ...

... make a fist with your hands ...

... and your heart goes *boom, boom, boom.*

Anger changes the way you see the world.
Everything seems **very unfair**.

Being angry makes you want to **scream, shout,** or **cry.**
You might want to **hit, bite,** or **kick** someone.

Waaah!

Being angry can make you feel sick.

There are lots of things you can do to help
when you feel you are getting angry.

Take deep, slow breaths. Do this until you feel calm.

Breathe **in**,
breathe **out**,
breathe **in**,
breathe **out!**

Count from 1 to 10 slowly out loud or
in your head. Can you count with Little Panda?

1, 2, 3, 4, 5, 6, 7, 8, 9, 10.

Look around you. Think about what you can you see.

Little Panda can see some clouds, a tree, and a car.
What else can she see?

It's not bad **to feel angry.**

But don't do anything mean
to other people while you
are angry.

Find a place where you feel safe, and you can be angry by yourself.

When you are in your safe place ...

...**jump** up and down...

...**dance** ...

...**bang** a drum...

...**clap** your hands ...

...**sing** loudly!

Run around if you can.

Thump your pillow or a soft cushion.

This will help you calm down.

When you feel better,
talk to someone you love.

Talk about what made
you angry and why it
made you feel that way.

Have a hug. Everyone feels better after a hug!

# Notes for parents and carers

All young children throw tantrums, get angry, and have meltdowns.
It's part of growing up. There are many ways parents, carers, and other trusted adults can help children understand and manage their anger.

- Never shout at or show your frustration to an angry child, as this just escalates the situation. Avoid confrontation.

- Make it clear that getting angry in itself is not a bad thing. Anger is a natural human emotion, and it can be a way to cope with frustration. It is how a child behaves when angry that needs to be discussed.

- You should lay out some guidelines. If your child is angry, they can go to a safe space (their room, the playroom) and scream, thump a pillow, or shout to let off steam. Be clear that hitting other people, biting, breaking things, spitting, and saying bad words is not allowed.

- Read through this book with your child. Talk about why Little Panda is getting angry and how she reacts. Discuss what makes your child angry. Being aware of what makes them angry means that a child can start to learn how to avoid that situation in the first place.

- Discuss why it is good to be able to control your anger. It is better if the child understands why there is a need to control anger, rather than just being told what to do.

- Read about the ways Little Panda can manage her anger. Discuss these with your child. Try some of the breathing and mindfulness exercises together.

- Reassure your child that you are always there for them, and no matter how angry they get you'll always love them. Hugs are a great healer!